THE DECISION WAS EASY

The Ground Truth About Safety Leadership

MARC D. MCGI[NNIS]

The Decision Was Easy
The Ground Truth about Safety Leadership
All Rights Reserved.
Copyright © 2019 Marc D. McGill
v1.0

The opinions expressed in this manuscript are solely the opinions of the author and do not represent the opinions or thoughts of the publisher. The author has represented and warranted full ownership and/or legal right to publish all the materials in this book.

This book may not be reproduced, transmitted, or stored in whole or in part by any means, including graphic, electronic, or mechanical without the express written consent of the publisher except in the case of brief quotations embodied in critical articles and reviews.

Outskirts Press, Inc.
http://www.outskirtspress.com

ISBN: 978-1-9772-1213-9

Cover Photo © 2019 www.gettyimages.com. All rights reserved - used with permission.

Outskirts Press and the "OP" logo are trademarks belonging to Outskirts Press, Inc.

PRINTED IN THE UNITED STATES OF AMERICA

TABLE OF CONTENTS

The Incident	1
If I Wouldn't Do It	7
It Became Easy	12
Safety First	15
Atta-Boy	21
What I Taught	25
What Next?	28

Introduction

After my incident in 1988, or what I will refer to as my personal "significant emotional event," I had a decision to make. If what I was currently living through was any measure of my future, something was going to have to change. As I was granted an inordinate amount of unwanted time, I found myself walking through the events, time after time, exploring what went wrong. The deep thoughts were rudely interrupted by the excruciating pain, called the typical burn "healing processes." In addition, I was told time after time how "lucky" I was I only suffered second degree burns – which, by the way, are the most painful and the most likely to get infected because the outer layer of the skin is destroyed revealing the raw nerve fibers. I didn't feel "lucky," but this word consumed me as I scrutinized what happened that made me so "lucky." I had convinced myself that behaviors back at the workplace would change before my return. After all, I was their leader and I was certain that my incident would be as emotional to my employees as it was to me.

Sixty days or so with my return, and I was amazed to find that the drivers for production and the workplace behaviors were still "business as usual."

I really want to be clear there was never any intention, by myself or any other employee, to put anyone in an unsafe situation or any potential exposure to any recognized hazard. Our efforts were motivated by maximizing production and minimizing downtime, just completing the job or task in minimal time. In hindsight, it was obvious we were heavily dependent on our "luck" to finish a day unharmed. We just didn't realize how much "luck" was on our side.

The day I returned to work was the day I realized the strength of a culture and the power that production in the tank has with boots on the ground folks. Workers closest to the wellhead feel all of the accountability for getting oil in the tanks and gas in the pipeline. Is it production then safety, or is it safety then production? I know, you're thinking that the choice seems easy. Well, it's not! For many boots on the ground folks in the oil and gas industry, it is something we struggle with every day. This short story brings to life the struggles I had in balancing production and safety.

The Decision Was Easy

I was once told, if I wouldn't do it, I couldn't stay,
So I did it and went on my way.
The decision was easy; I had a family to raise!
It became easy, safety was just a delay.
It only took a minute, what could it hurt.
The decision was easy; I had a family to raise!
"Safety first" they would say.
"Oh and finish by the end of the day."
The decision was easy; I had a family to raise!
"Atta-boy, whatever it takes."
Safety then Production, or is it Production then Safety.
The decision was easy; I had a family to raise!
Bypassing safety became easy;
Bypassing safety was what I taught.
The decision was easy; I had a family to raise!
Burning and hurting; nothing left but dying.
Life insurance paid.
The decision was easy; I had a family to raise!

© *Marc McGill*

The Incident

A huge flash of fire in the middle of darkness. Just a few minutes prior, I remember explaining the procedure for lighting a wellhead flare to Kevin, one of my employees. Because his gut was telling him that something wasn't right, Kevin had taken the time to stop lighting wellhead flares. Each flare he lit resulted in some flash back, when the flame recesses to an unwanted position, typically toward you. He stopped work and drove back to the facility to express his hesitation in continuing.

My response to him when he arrived was, "It's simple. C'mon, I'll show you." I now know that the production pressures coupled with the influence from my personal risk tolerance, not safety, were driving my actions. I'm just thankful that my action put only me at risk and not Kevin. I could have easily pushed back on Kevin and encouraged him to just light one more flare, but I was the kind of leader that was willing to *walk the walk*. We both went to the field, a remote location where individual pump jacks are located, where I attempted to light the flare.

October nights in Illinois are usually damp and cool; this night was no different. It's ironic how we remember the painful details of significant events but on any other ordinary day, we remember almost nothing. I remember I wore blue jean pants and a long- sleeved shirt, sleeves rolled up to my elbows. The shirt was 50% cotton and 50% polyester, and I can still remember it was blue in color with some sort of pattern of tan stripes. I was also wearing a ball cap, tan in color with a blue bill; I believe it had a local vendor's name. Vendor hats are something easily collected in the oil and gas industry. My choices of wardrobe were less than adequate for the activity I was about to do since they only aggravated the intensity of the burns. Flame Resistant Clothing (FRC) was not something we were issued or wore.

Fog and darkness were two additional hazards this night. I can remember the visibility in front of me was maybe forty feet. Fog lingered close to the ground, giving off a feeling of a moist heaviness, as if I were walking through sludge. On top of that, there was complete darkness, not even a glimpse of light from the moon available. The situation required me to demonstrate my resourcefulness to Kevin, so I proceeded to use the light emitted from the pickup truck headlights.

You're probably thinking, "Are you serious?" Yes, working by the headlights at individual well locations is often practiced in onshore oil and gas operations. At this point, in my mind, everything was aligning perfectly, especially since it had now been about twelve hours since the gas plant had been down. "Down" is clearly defined in our world as "no production," which means "no revenue." The warning signs were there; in fact, they were almost screaming at me, and yet, I continued to move forward with the task. I am certain that the last "sign" was the "sign" that influenced my decision to move forward. Just another "lucky" day.

The task called for lighting an individual well flare, a two-inch piece of pipe standing vertical about fifteen feet in the air. The two-inch pipe was connected to the casing of the wellbore about fifty feet away. The procedure I was taught—unwritten, by the way—required us to close off the two-inch valve at the wellhead, isolating the flare from the casing. This closure should stop any flow of gas into the two-inch pipe and exiting through the flare. Once closed, one person ties a rag on the end of a fifteen-foot pole, ignites the rag and holds it near the outlet of the flare in preparation for the flare to ignite while a second person slowly opens the two-inch valve slowing releasing gas to allow for ignition at the outlet. Once the outlet ignites, the individual would back out with the pole while the two-inch valve is continually opened. The process is simple, quite similar to lighting a gas grill, except the amount of gas being controlled by the two-inch valve has the capability of supplying a year's worth of heat to your home. Simple, especially since we'd done it a thousand times.

However, this night was different. I'm not sure if the valve was leaking or if the damp, cool, and foggy night had prevented the gas that was being released into the atmosphere, prior to us closing the two-inch valve, from dissipating. Keep in mind that before we shut the two-inch valve, gas was being vented from the two-inch flare pipe into the atmosphere; it was not ignited. Anyway, I tied the rag on the end of the pole as I was taught, ignited it, and made my way to the outlet of the flare pipe—pole in hand and the rag in flames. Before I could reach the outlet, still several feet to go, it happened! A huge flash of flames must have been at least a hundred-foot radius or more around the flare. It lasted no more than just a few seconds—a few seconds that would impact what would seem like an eternity of hospital stays, doctor's visits, wound care, pain management, internal therapy, and my family.

Not only was the wardrobe I had chosen not fire-resistant but I also was not wearing a monitor to identify if a flammable atmosphere was present. In fact, we were never issued such equipment from the company. It was evident there was a flammable atmosphere—my 50% cotton and 50% polyester shirt was mostly gone leaving only the collar, the rolled-up portion of the sleeves around my elbows, and the front center placket. My vendor ball cap was now a visor.

Without speaking much, it was obvious that Kevin was now the designated driver, so we quickly got in the pickup truck, knowing the end destination was the hospital. While he began to drive, I remember telling myself, *It can't be that bad; the flash only lasted a few seconds.* Even with all that had occurred, I was thinking through tomorrow's activities, planning the next morning. As we drove by the gas plant on our way to the hospital, I thought, *I will be back in morning and will get production back on line.* I quickly situated myself where my entire upper body stuck out of the passenger side window in an effort to get some relief from the air movement. Afraid to look down, I worked up the courage to take a quick peek and recall seeing a flake like substance coming off my upper body and suddenly realizing why I was reluctant to look in the first place. The flake, now flapping in the wind, wasn't my shirt, but my skin. The pain relief the wind initially provided didn't last long. The pain was beginning to creep in, increasing each minute that followed. My story was beginning to be real; it only lasted a few seconds. Could this really be the end?

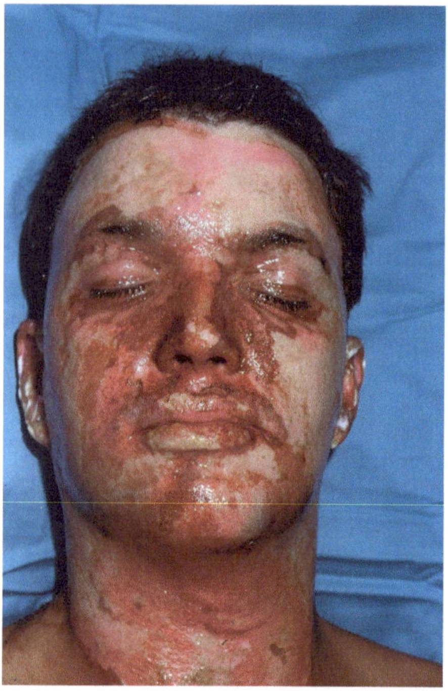

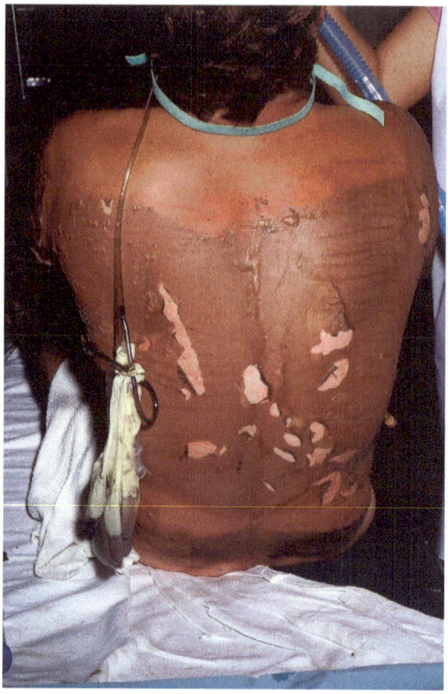

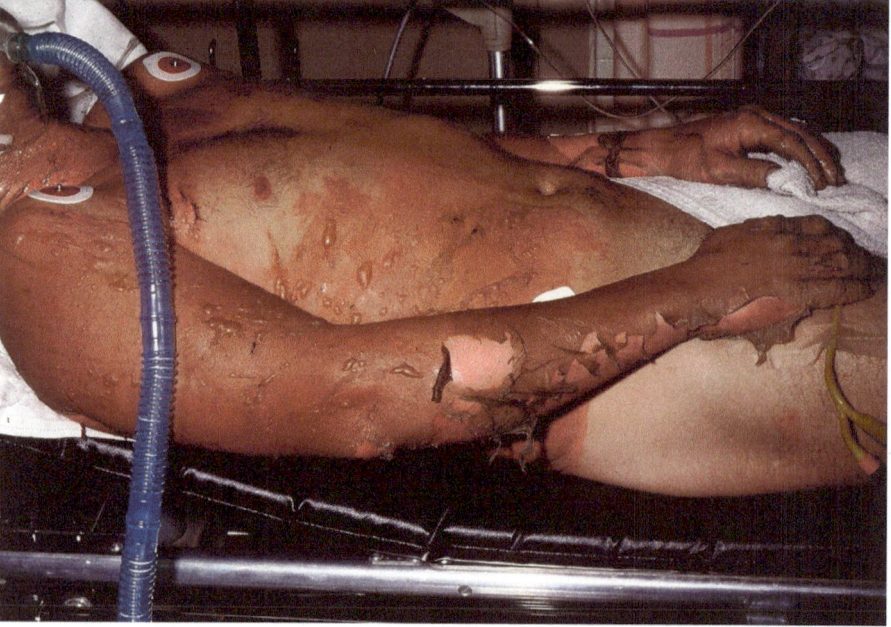

IF I WOULDN'T DO IT

I was a production supervisor, the position where boots on the ground started, managing an onshore natural gas processing facility. All of my knowledge and experience up until this point had all been gained on the job. *Lessons learned* and *lessons experienced* – two different things, from my perspective. *Lessons learned* are generally lessons that others have experienced and are willing to share. More importantly, you don't know the individual or have an awareness of the location where the event occurred. *Lessons learned* can provide value if the individual delivering the message has some knowledge of the task and is willing and able to personalize the message. Personalizing someone else's story is difficult and is not often a skillset an individual possesses.

Lessons experienced, on the other hand, are events I have a personal connection with. Usually I am directly involved, but it could also be something that occurred with an individual or location that I know well or have some direct influence over. *Lessons experienced* tend to be more influential because we can personalize the message or story. The details are real, and the listener can feel the connection and authenticity through the storyteller. Fortunately and unfortunately, the oil and gas industry is full of *lessons experienced* and individuals with the mindset that learning from our mistakes is just part of the job.

I used to make excuses for this mindset, as many of us do. I was fearless and bulletproof; after all, this is a risky industry that requires at-risk behaviors, and injury was just a consequence of it. It wasn't until years later that I realized my behavior was a result of my need to prove my skills, knowledge and experience in order to do my job. You see, because I was fairly new in the industry, with minimal industry knowledge and experience, I had to offset this with a performance ethic of "get 'er done," no matter what.

> "I was once told, if I wouldn't do it, I couldn't stay/So I did it and went on my way."

This was simply not true; that is, these exact words were never spoken to me, but the actions I observed and the words I heard might as well have spelled this out to me exactly as I've stated here. The environment I worked in created an atmosphere where I felt if I didn't get the job finished, then someone else would. As a reward, those individuals would then get what I wanted: more money and a promotion. My strategy worked, at least until the day of the incident. I had begun my career in the oil and gas industry as a gas plant operator, and at the time of the incident I was the gas plant supervisor. There were four years of lessons experienced between the two positions. I got the job done and was rewarded accordingly.

It may seem strange, but I feel it is important for the reader to understand that many individuals in many different industries are not always promoted for years of experience and verified knowledge, or what I refer to as competency. My education, as with many of the boots on the ground folks in the oil and gas industry, became the "School of Hard Knocks." These are the lessons experienced I discussed earlier. It seemed to be the only way for me to gain knowledge and advance my career. Many of the individuals I knew in the industry were no different. What I didn't understand, at that time, was that my personal risk tolerance was a huge factor in accurately identifying the risks and hazards I faced. At the time of the incident, I was the leader in terms of position. But my entire team was young, bullet proof and truly believed we could out work, outperform anyone else in our industry.

When you're young in age and your appearance is even more deceiving, I have found that you make every effort to offset people's impressions of "You're just a kid, and you don't know yet." I offset these impressions with my overconfidence and possibly even pretending to know things I didn't. My perspective was that the oil and gas industry was a man's industry, and if you showed weakness you wouldn't last long. In other words, even if you don't know, you pretend to know and just jump in and do your job—my pretended competency. At least, back in 1988, that is how I thought the industry was and how I was wired. In turn, this belief forced me into situations where I had little to no knowledge about how to proceed but did anyway. Each of these situations created my lessons experienced. Even twenty-six years later, I can immediately identify with individuals with similar behaviors.

Twenty-five years after this event, I was participating in a presentation to a group of crude oil transportation drivers and during the question and answer session, an individual from the audience was targeted with a question from one of the other presenters. This individual from the audience appeared to be the youngest individual in the room, and I am sure this is why he was sought out to answer the question. In my opinion, he could not have been a day over twenty years old. The question directed to the young individual was "How long have you worked for your company?" I just knew what was going to come out of his mouth, maybe before he even knew what he was going to say. I seem to have a knack of putting myself in the shoes of the boots on the ground folk. Plus, I have seen this type of individual before; years ago, I saw this individual every time I looked in the mirror.

He said, "I have only been with this company for four months, but I have been in the oil and gas industry for four years." Then it came, what I was expecting him to say: "But I have done everything!" I got a terrible feeling in my gut. My mind just kind of rewound back to the late 1980s. I wanted to ask him a million questions and to explore his thinking. Of course, I didn't. The one thing this young man had that I didn't was individuals willing to share their lessons experienced. You see, I had just spent forty-five minutes prior to this comment sharing my story, this story. Through my poem I had described my young, inexperienced and bulletproof behaviors that often drove my decisions. I explained the opportunities we all have to work safely and to make good decisions. Yet, this young man was not having any of it. I thought about this since and thus I have added to my story this chapter describing my fight within, my fight to prove my industry competency, even at my young age.

It Became Easy

I mentioned earlier, how I realized the power culture has on an organization, a group of individuals or a single individual. I later understood this culture was being driven, unintentionally, by the organization and then ultimately by me. I was always very successful in influencing everyone around me. I didn't know it at the time, but I was creating the culture. This is something that all front-line supervisors should accept early in their careers: you create your team's culture. My drive to do a good job, unfortunately, clouded my judgment.

> "It became easy, safety was just a delay.
> It only took a minute, what could it hurt"

Several hours earlier, the day of the incident, the morning started with the entire facility shut down. This wasn't the first time I'd had to talk with the boss and give him the news that the plant was down, which meant, in his words, "no production." This conversation about downtime and why it occurred was always difficult for most, but I learned to master the ability to tell them exactly what they wanted to hear. I just refocused the conversation on what seemed to be most important to him: bringing the facility, along with production, back on line. I was able to commit my team and me with an actual timeframe when the plant would be back on line. This became easy; after all, we were all driven by our production performance. I viewed the front-line leadership position's role as the filter. I filtered details of various problems to senior leadership, and I filtered details of various communications from management to the boots on the ground folks.

Managing problems and solving problems was what they paid me for. In the back of my mind, I was saying, "If I cannot solve problems, then I will just be replaced." I was twenty-nine years of age, and I didn't come to be in this position, production supervisor, by bringing problems to senior leadership. I got this position by managing problems and keeping downtime to a minimum. No matter what!

The commitment I made to leadership to have the plant back on line before the end of the day became the driver of our decisions for the entire day. You can use words like "taking a short cut," or "cutting corners," but whatever the term, we were being driven by time and some, if not most, decisions would be driven by this commitment. When you're driven by time, it is easy to simplify the most complicated tasks or jobs. This day was no different. The facility was down, and the entire crew knew, even without my saying it, that we would need to be back on line by the end of the day. Along with this, it just made sense that while the equipment was all down, we might as well perform the maintenance that was due in just a few weeks. If we could complete this maintenance today, during this unscheduled downtime, then we could actually skip the next scheduled maintenance that would otherwise result in additional downtime. Simple: look at the next scheduled maintenance and complete as much as we could now; at least, all of the critical tasks. All of the other minor tasks could be pushed to another scheduled maintenance. We had done this in the past and it worked. Besides, uptime was part of our annual performance evaluations and bonuses. We did it so much in the past, without incident, that it became expected; it became easy.

Safety First

"Safety First" was something I struggled with for years. I am sure I could be quoted as saying, "Safety first was just something management has to say; what else would they say, safety last?" It is not that my intentions were to work unsafely, but let's face it, the oil and gas industry was oozing with hazards and staffed with at-risk individuals to manage those hazards. Not a really good combination. I never did anything I felt would have resulted in an injury, but I did take some chances.

Back to management; just consider the term "daily production meetings," for example. In the oil and gas industry, daily production meetings are held between management and field operations; the main topic is the production of oil in the tank or gas in the pipeline. This is probably not any different than the production output of any other industry; after all, production does pay the bills. Early in my career, the only discussion around safety, during these production meetings, was when someone got injured, resulting in the production being halted. This doesn't mean that leadership didn't care about the safety of its personnel, because they did; it is something that I didn't grasp at the time. Now I believe that leadership just didn't know how to properly communicate the importance of safe operations. It wasn't until way later in my career that I understood why leadership didn't feel it was necessary to communicate safe operations. Many leaders just assume safe operations is the ultimate driver. After all, no one comes to work to get hurt; everybody knows that!

The past thirteen years, I have been in a safety leadership role. What I have determined, and there are exceptions, is that most leaders have not been properly trained on how to have the safety conversations. "How" is the key word! Why is it important and necessary to have the safety conversations? As I stated above, there isn't anyone who comes to work to get injured, and if/when an injury does occur, it is communicated as an accident. All of our childhoods have been shaped to believe an accident is just an unintentional, non-preventable event. Thinking back, I was an active child, or as my mom would probably say, "hell on two feet." There were numerous times I broke something, a lamp or a dish, and Mom would just say, "Oh that is ok, it was just an accident." Do accidents just happen? Are they even preventable? How does that correlate with the assumption that safety is just assumed? Earlier I talked about *lessons experienced;* this message, or the lack thereof, is what drives your culture:

"Safety first," they would say.
"Oh, and finish by the end of the day."
The decision was easy; I had a family to raise!

It was many years later until I was able to understand safety from the perspective of senior leadership. I was able to successfully make the transition from boots on the ground to a senior leadership position. As I stated earlier, I began my career in the oil and gas industry as a gas plant operator. Twenty-six years later, I hold the position of director of environmental, health, safety, and regulatory. I believe that leadership truly believes in "safety first" but will never achieve safe operations unless they accept three things. First, leaders cannot believe that accidents just happen. Second, leaders cannot believe that safety just happens for boots on the ground activity. Most of all, leaders must be good at creating the safety conversation.

Lessons learned for the reader: Whether you're a boots on the ground employee or a member of leadership, safety conversations between the two groups are necessary for a safe operation. In order to prevent an event, an injury, or an accident (yes, an accident is preventable), you must learn how to have a safety conversation. Maybe more important is *when* to have the safety conversation; this is more difficult than it probably seems. As a member of leadership, you must be engaged in a conversation about the upcoming work activity and be willing to drill down deeper into any specific task. For example, during the conversation you ask, "Have you identified the hazards or risks associated with the work activity?" You can expect a reply from the boots on the ground folks: "Yes." Most leaders will stop here and without knowing it, may be promoting an unsafe/at-risk behavior and ultimately creating a culture of at-risk behavior. I mean, how do you know what "yes" means, unless you ask?

My experiences are full of stories of me filtering-up. For example, if I had a facility down, I knew all I needed to say was, "No worries, we will have it back on line by the end of the day." Ultimately, that was what leadership wanted to hear, and I knew that. I also knew that if I responded with that message, I would drive the leadership conversation on to the next topic. As leaders, we cannot allow this to happen. Don't stop there; you must force yourself to get engaged with follow-up questions: "What are the hazards and risks identified?" "How do you plan on mitigating each?" As leaders, we should keep in mind that middle management/supervisors get in this internal struggle with themselves on how much information do they need to tell the boss? Believe me, they will share all the information, if asked! Leaders, it is our responsibility to remove the filter by asking the questions; it's about the job, the task, and the people. As I stated earlier, the conversation that I believe is necessary to achieve a safe operation is difficult. It is difficult as leaders to train ourselves when and how to have the conversation.

Now let's look through the lenses of the front-line supervisor. The front-line supervisor will find the questions uncomfortable. After all, he or she was hired to make these decisions and often will feel that you don't trust their experience, their knowledge, or both. Be sure you explain your reason for the questions; it is because you believe in "Safety First," and you consider these types of conversation valuable.

I remember a conversation with an individual higher in the organization, who used the term "the bigger brain." It was used in the context of the fact that getting more individuals involved in a conversation sooner rather than later is better. Now we can agree or disagree about this and head off down a few trails, but his point was that if he is ultimately responsible, then he should be allowed to listen to the reasoning surrounding a decision and have an opportunity to get more involved in the detail. Lesson Learned: Don't hesitate to get the bigger brain involved. As the conversations occur and there are explanations as to why, the supervisors will learn, and in most cases, encourage these types of conversations. After all, these types of conversations build affinity, allowing for both groups to fully understand each other's perspective for safety and create a culture for safe operations.

Go back to my story; I talked about how I could influence the conversation with my boss when having conversations around downtime. I felt I was telling leadership what they wanted to know. I wasn't so sure that their expectation was *safety first*; we rarely discussed work activity from a safety perspective. What if our conversation, the morning of my incident, would have been different? I could have started the conversation with discussions about all of the work required to complete the repairs and maintenance. Leadership could have asked more detailed questions about the repairs, forcing and encouraging me to talk about the risks associated with completing the activity. Just maybe, after this type of conversation, there could have been an alignment on what and how much work we needed to complete during this repair. Maybe, just maybe, my event would never have occurred.

Atta-Boy

There are perils of employee recognition. Have you ever recognized someone for a "job well done"? What was your reasoning for the recognition, the final product? We all do it; we are focusing on the result without any clue about the risks or shortcuts an individual took to achieve this success. For example, you send your teenager in town for an item you desperately need, and when they return you acknowledge how pleased you are, good job! Now let's consider that the trip took half the time it should have. What have we really recognized? Speeding and coasting through stop signs? We intentionally gave recognition for result of getting what you needed and unintentionally gave recognition that it was okay to take a shortcut if it is really necessary or urgent:

> "Atta-boy, whatever it takes."
> Safety then Production, or is it Production then Safety?
> The decision was easy; I had a family to raise!

This unintentional action resulting in these unforeseen consequences is how we create our culture. I mentioned earlier that a front-line supervisor creates his or her team's culture. The problem with creating a culture is that most of the time, it was never part of any plan. As I remember back, there were endless examples of how my actions created a culture that production was king and unintentionally put safety in the background. I think it is important to provide two different examples that demonstrate how front-line supervisors demonstrate or encourage at-risk behaviors that create a culture that fosters unsafe operations. First, I can remember one of my employees, David, informing me that it was going to be necessary to shut down the plant and replace a regulator. I said, "No that is not necessary; come with me and I will show you how we can do it." In my second example, I didn't personally demonstrate the at-risk behavior but promoted the at-risk behavior. Have you ever said, "Don't even tell me how you got that job finished?" Ever remember a time when crews were on location attempting a job that you purposely chose not to visit? Why? Because you didn't want to see how they were attempting a specific task, a task that you suspected was just a little risky.

Both examples are how a front-line supervisor just supported and recognized how important production was and that it was okay to cut a few corners. After all, nobody got hurt. As a front-line supervisor, this can be the most valuable *lessons experienced* that I can share with you. If you remember, I said earlier that as I spent time off work in the burn center and at home, I had no doubt that work practices, back at the plant, had changed. I could not have been more wrong. This is when I really understood the power a culture has on a workforce. Wow, I had created a culture, an unplanned creation of a culture that allowed and supported production as our priority. If you are also recognizing these types of behaviors, you too will realize that this is not what you intended to do. I was lucky; my crew didn't get burned, I did! I spent the next fifteen years working to create a culture where we recognized individuals for safe operations and safe behaviors. That is correct: four years to unintentionally create an at-risk culture and fifteen years to plan and create the opposite. It is not easy!

I want to leave you with one last memory of how simple recognition can unintentionally create the wrong culture. As a leader, have you ever made it to the field, the rig, or the job site and you were asked to deliver a message to the boots on the ground folks? Did you ever deliver this message by giving a message similar to "This team is doing an excellent job, maximizing production and keeping expenses to a minimum? I want to thank all of you for your hard work it is much appreciated. Keep up the good work and as always work safe." So you stopped by a worksite that you were unfamiliar with, a worksite where the front-line supervisor is driven by output and as I shared in my story above, allowed for corners to be cut. What was the message that your conversation sent? What was the culture you were helping to create? That is correct: if the culture was that production was king and so far they had been lucky and no one had been injured, your communication supported their efforts. *Lessons experienced*: plan for your message, know the worksite performance, know the front-line supervisors, and most of all have conversations with the boots on the ground folks and feel what they are experiencing.

WHAT I TAUGHT

I encourage you to read through the poem again. Can you visualize how the culture was created—unplanned but well executed? It all started with a hard-working, high spirited young man who had no idea that outperforming leadership expectations would keep his job. How easy it was to focus only on the outcome, no matter what, jumping into a world of influencing the outcome by filtering information and allowing justifications for why leadership had to say "Safety First." Leadership, through promotions and bonuses, unintentionally recognized this entire endeavor as acceptable. This leads me to the stage in my life when I begin teaching everything I have learned to this point—all of which, as I would learn years later, was mistaken for success. I was two years into my oil and gas career and already been promoted to facility supervisor.

My experience led me to build a team of individuals

who were hard working, knowledgeable with equipment, and driven to prove their worth. Keep in mind that by worth I don't mean dollars; you proved your worth by being willing to work long and hard hours, focusing on results. A team bond was formed and we focused on the results:

> **Bypassing safety became easy;**
> **Bypassing safety was what I taught.**
> **The decision was easy; I had a family to raise!**

In reality, this is the part of my career that is the most disappointing. I was totally unaware how powerful that culture was until days, even months after my return to work following my incident. In fact, it was a constant struggle internally not to allow the pressures of focusing on production to control my decisions. I know that I often fell back into the trap, but the difference was that I was able to recognize what I had done. I was able to continually battle this internal struggle—at least anyway until I began to see the small wins. These were wins for the entire group; four gas monitors, permit to work, and a first ever safety manual. It was happening; the culture was swinging. *Lessons learned*: changing culture is all-day, every day and requires oversight and continuous conversations. Through failures, I now understand that creating a safety culture isn't easy and doesn't just happen.

I can remember later in my career that I worked very hard to purposely create a safety culture that believed and lived that safe operations was king, not production. Again,

I want to stress that it will never allow you to let up on the effort, but there are good wins along the way that make every effort worthwhile. For example, I was attending a meeting with various members of front-line supervisors from various disciplines whose purpose was to share lessons experienced across asset boundaries. As a safety professional, I never once had to enter the conversation. Safe operations just seemed to be a part of every conversation, and the ownership that was being caused was incomparable to any other time in my career! I remember feeling it was just like when your child graduates from college and they are just all grown up with adult thoughts and conversations. Doesn't mean we ever let up; safe operations is all day, every day!

What Next?

As you and I continue on this journey, we should continue to learn, share, and have the right conversations. We must train ourselves to listen for indicators, words or phrases, which steer a conversation toward output—product in the tank. Don't get alarmed when you notice yourself heading that direction; it will happen. When this happens, you should congratulate yourself. You are now learning what safe operations is all about; self-awareness to recognize when more conversation is necessary. Key words or phrases to listen for:

- Many workers will lead their supervisor in to a trusting compromise by stating something like, **"Don't worry, I got this."** The worker knows there are other items to discuss, so it is very easy for the supervisor to trust the worker and move on. Many times, the worker doesn't know how he or she "has it" but has just committed themselves or their teams to complete the task. What the supervisor should respond with is something like, "Good; let's go through your thinking on how you plan to complete this task. Maybe we can help." This statement will drive more conversations with more details and should open an opportunity for the supervisor to recognize any at-risk behavior and to slow the activity down.

- This statement is really similar to the discussion above; however, the activity has already been completed: "**We had a small problem last night but everything is back on line.**" With the activity completed, as supervisors, we almost never question what the problem was or how the activity was completed. This is a great opportunity to learn from the past and change direction for future similar events. There are two possible outcomes from saying, "Let's discuss the what and how." 1) Everything was completed risk free, which would be followed up with some sort of recognition, or 2) There were risks not properly mitigated, in which case there is an opportunity to establish better expectation for future decisions. Nothing happens if we do not take a moment to discuss.
- When we hear something like **"I'm not sure, but the mechanic said everything was working,"** the worker doesn't really want to talk about the activity—and why would the supervisor ask? After all, he or she already knows the worker doesn't know. This is a great opportunity to bring others into the conversation. Everyone has a cell phone these days, just pause and give the

worker an opportunity to call the mechanic and include him or her in the conversation.

- As supervisors, we should stay away from statements like **"Do you think you can be finished soon?" "We really need to get this on by the end of the day,"** or **"We will have production back on line soon."** All of these types of statements lead our workers to satisfy our need to "hurry." Who wants to disappoint their supervisor? These types of statements all require additional statements such as, "This doesn't mean to take any short cuts or to cut any corners" or "If it takes an extra day, it just does."

www.ingramcontent.com/pod-product-compliance
Lightning Source LLC
Chambersburg PA
CBHW040253220526
45473CB00001B/469